Bee... ...and
Overtures

Roger Fiske

ROGER FISKE

BEETHOVEN
Concertos & Overtures
BBC MUSIC GUIDES

ARIEL MUSIC
BBC PUBLICATIONS

Published by BBC Publications
A division of BBC Enterprises Ltd
35 Marylebone High Street, London W1M 4AA

ISBN 0 563 20482 6

First published 1970
Reprinted 1975, 1977, 1979
First published in Ariel Music 1986

Typeset in 10/11 pt Garamond by Phoenix Photosetting, Chatham
Printed in England by Mackays of Chatham Ltd

Contents

The Classical Concerto

The classical concerto emerged only a short time before Beethoven was born (which was in 1770), and to him its newness must have been one of its most intriguing attributes. Early examples seldom reach our concert-halls, and it would be easy to conclude that there was an unbridgeable chasm between the keyboard concertos Bach wrote in, perhaps, the 1730s and those Mozart wrote a mere fifty years later. In a sense there was a chasm. But there was also a bridge, and inevitably Beethoven was much better informed about it than we are today.

So far as keyboard concertos are concerned, the most important event in the transitional or bridging period was the switch from the harpsichord to the piano. The harpsichord lost its popularity mainly because it could not be played expressively with gradations of loudness; however hard you pushed down one of the keys the sound was the same, whereas its rival could be played either *piano* or *forte* as its name implied. Also the harpsichord was an unsatisfactory concerto instrument because it could not compete with an orchestra in carrying power, and for this reason most composers never wrote concertos for it. Bach and his sons did so, but their harpsichord concertos were chamber music rather than orchestral music; they probably expected the accompanying 'orchestra' to consist of no more than four or five players.

In 1749, just before he died, Bach saw and played one of the newfangled pianos, but neither he nor Handel ever wrote for the instrument. As their design improved, pianos became more and more of a commercial proposition, and they were soon putting music publishers in a quandary. If keyboard music was written with dynamic contrasts, their harpsichord-owning customers would be alienated. Pianos can hardly have outnumbered harpsichords in the home much before the last decade of the century, and until then publishers preferred to describe their keyboard music as for harpsichord even when those who wrote it intended it for the piano; dynamic contrasts that were impossible on the harpsichord had to be omitted. When Bach's youngest son, Johann Christian, arrived in London about 1762 he quickly published as his Op. 1 a set of six concertos for 'clavecin' and strings, but by the 1770s when he published his second and third sets of keyboard concertos enough people in England had bought pianos for the music to be described as for 'cembalo' *or* pianoforte. Publishers did not drop the word harpsichord (or its French or Italian equivalents) from their title-pages until the end of the century. Even Beethoven's Op. 2 piano sonatas were offered as 'pour le clavecin ou piano-forte', though the most cursory glance must have revealed explosive sforzandi that were quite impossible on the harpsichord.

Beethoven was growing up during this social changeover: the replacing of one instrument in the home by another. He must have known old-fashioned people in Bonn who deplored the harpsichord's decline, and this probably made him the more eager to exploit the excitingly dramatic possibilities of its successor. From the first he went out of his way to make his own keyboard music unplayable on the harpsichord; his innumerable dynamic contrasts are in some degree a reaction against the immediate past. He was the first great composer who never wrote for the harpsichord. Mozart, who was fourteen years older, had done so in youth, but in maturity intended all his keyboard music for the piano. Indeed it was Mozart who first developed the piano concerto into a fully satisfying art form. The examples he wrote in the 1780s, when Beethoven was in his teens, are among the chief wonders of the classical repertoire. But Beethoven did even more than Mozart to turn the concerto into a major attraction at concerts.

The late baroque composers, such as Vivaldi and Bach, had usually begun their concertos with a movement of considerable length in which the main theme, some sixteen bars in length, was played by the orchestra at the beginning and the end. In between there were passages of figuration for the soloist punctuated by bits of the main theme in various related keys on the orchestra. These passages provided an element of contrast without offering a positively memorable tune. Only in his Concerto for Two Violins did Bach anticipate classical methods and use two contrasting themes in a movement.

By 1760 contrasting themes were becoming usual in both symphonies and concertos, but structurally the two kinds of music were not much alike. In symphonies the first and (sometimes) the last movement were in a binary form with repeat marks in the middle demanding that the exposition of the themes should be played twice. But there were normally no repeat marks in concertos because there had been none in their baroque models. Composers lengthened the orchestral opening to include contrasting themes and then brought in the soloist for a very free repeat of this opening material. In a sense the exposition comes twice, but the two versions are very different in detail. Beethoven, following Mozart, sometimes introduced an important new theme in the soloist's exposition that had not occurred in the orchestral exposition. More rarely, he let the orchestra have a contrasting theme that did not come again until the recapitulation. In extreme cases, for instance in Mozart's A major Violin Concerto, the two expositions seem to have very little relationship. The orchestral tutti following the soloist's exposition was normally in the dominant and it led to a freely modulating section in which the soloist displayed his technique in quick arpeggios and runs. Before about 1775 these were thought to be of sufficient interest on their own, but later it was usual for the orchestra to interpose quiet fragments of the main theme behind the figuration passages. The result resembled the development section in a symphony, but in a concerto the development of the themes was subsidiary to the soloist's display. This music led to a recapitulation with all the themes normally in the tonic. Then came a pause mark, which indicated that the soloist could extemporise a cadenza; this ended on a trill by way of warning to the orchestra to be ready for the final tutti.

So complex a structure was not evolved in a moment, and its gradual development can be seen in the three sets of keyboard concertos by J. C. Bach. (These were to a large extent the models for Mozart's piano concertos, which in turn were to a large extent the models for Beethoven's.) In his Op. 1 set two of the six start like symphonies with movements in two sections, each of which is to be repeated. None of the first movements has a clearly defined second subject. But in the Op. 7 set, written about the year that Beethoven was born, second subjects are not only in evidence but already have that feminine lyricism which was to be associated with them for a hundred years and more. Bach sometimes keeps such a tune back for the soloist's exposition, and when he does the music must have, so to speak, two second subjects, for there has already been one in the orchestral exposition. In such movements it is more sensible to speak of the second-subject group.

Mozart chose to keep the orchestral exposition in his concertos entirely in the tonic, and thereby he established a convention. J. C. Bach had usually adopted the same scheme, but he sometimes modulated for the second subject in both expositions, as did Haydn in his Piano Concerto in D and Beethoven in his very early Piano Concerto in E flat, written at about the age of 14, and in the C minor, Op. 37. In the first movement of the latter he appeared to think better of what he had done; though the orchestra introduces the second subject in E flat Beethoven is careful not to establish the key too firmly and he soon has the orchestra repeating the same tune in the tonic. Tovey[1] felt that at this point he had escaped error only by the skin of his teeth, but in fact

1 *Essays in Musical Analysis*, iii (London, 1936), p. 71.

9

he was doing very much what J. C. Bach had done in his E flat Concerto, Op. 13 no. 6.

J. C. Bach invariably introduced his soloist with the first subject, the one which the orchestra had played at the start. Mozart increasingly preferred to introduce his soloist in new and somewhat improvisatory material; it was often a dozen bars or more before this led back to the first subject. Only one of J. C. Bach's 'London' concertos has any thematic development in the freely modulating section after the two expositions; even Mozart's concertos seldom show thematic development until the 1780s.

Slow movements were much simpler in design than first movements, and often suggested an operatic aria with the soloist taking the place of the singer. Either the orchestra alone or the soloist alone could start the movement. If an opportunity for extemporising a cadenza was allowed near the end, it was understood that such a cadenza should be short and expressive rather than long and flamboyant as in first movements.

Unlike the symphony, the classical concerto never expanded into four movements, no doubt because its baroque models had only three. Mozart sometimes ended his earlier concertos with a movement in minuet style or with one that included a minuet episode in the middle, but he did not do so in his mature music. Beethoven never saw the minuet as suitable material for a concerto, and his finales were all in rondo form; usually the soloist introduced the main subject.

Throughout the twentieth century it has been accepted that the symphony is the 'highest' instrumental form, and that the concerto, however fascinating it may be, is in some degree inferior. The belief that display is incompatible with the finest inspiration may have something to do with the theory, but it is not a theory Mozart would have welcomed; nor would Beethoven in his younger days. For Mozart the concerto was a more fecund form than the symphony. The composer usually had more control over the performance of a concerto, for more often than not he had written it for himself to play. In Beethoven's time performances might be either with a private orchestra in some palace or mansion, or with an ad hoc orchestra at a public subscription concert, though it must be stressed that by our standards concerts of any kind were very few. A subscription concert was normally organised by a composer, who canvassed subscriptions, wrote all or most of the music, paid the performers and pocketed the profits. As there was no conductor with a baton, a concerto was the only way a composer could focus attention on himself. He set the tempo at the start with his hand or violin-bow, and joined in the orchestral exposition if the ensemble seemed uncertain. Dittersdorf, who was a good violinist, wrote almost all his concertos for violin, and Dussek, who was a good pianist, wrote all his for piano. Haydn wrote comparatively few concertos because he had no great confidence in his abilities as a performer, and we shall see that when Beethoven realised that his deafness made it impossible for him to play piano concertos in public he stopped writing them.

Mozart must have been one of the first composers to write concertos for an instrument he did not play, and he invariably did so because a friend asked him to. When he composed his Clarinet Concerto for Stadler, it is unlikely that he expected or got any financial reward, but the certainty that such a work would be played and heard was for him a sufficient stimulus.

Concertos were never published in full score in the eighteenth century; because there was no conductor in the modern sense, a full score was not needed. A student could study the orchestration of a concerto he admired only if he made a score himself from the separate parts or if he managed to borrow one in manuscript. We must not overstate the influence of one work on another at this period. Beethoven certainly knew Mozart's Piano Concerto in D minor; he wrote cadenzas for it. But he probably knew well only the piano part; he can have had very few opportunities of hearing the work with orchestra.

The Early Piano Concertos

It is unlikely that Beethoven had had a sight of any Mozart concerto in 1784 when he composed his early Piano Concerto in E flat. What he wrote survives only as a piano solo with the orchestral sections included in piano arrangement. There is no indication of what the orchestra was doing while the soloist was playing.[1] Beethoven's father wrote on the autograph, 'composé par Louis van Beethoven âgé de douze ans', but in fact Beethoven was two years older; his father was bending the truth in the forlorn hope that the boy would be accepted as a child-prodigy. But, as this concerto reveals, Beethoven was a skilful youth rather than a Mozartian wonder-boy. The piano part is difficult, and so full of figuration clichés that one suspects he had been set the task of writing something really 'pianistic'. Certainly the orchestra did not get much of his attention. The slow movement is poor, but the finale has a pleasant theme in the style of Haydn, and a spirited second episode in the minor. We shall find that the latter is a characteristic of nearly all Beethoven's concerto rondos. The numerous dynamic contrasts in his solo part also point the way ahead.

Haydn passed through Bonn on his way to England, and was so impressed by what he was shown of Beethoven's music that he agreed to give him lessons when he got back to Vienna. The Elector of Cologne offered to finance Beethoven's education while he was there. The lessons took place in 1792-3, and when Haydn realised his pupil was unduly pressed for money, he wrote to the Elector asking him to help Beethoven more generously; as evidence of his progress he enclosed, among other works, an oboe concerto Beethoven had written. The Elector wrote back to say that the concerto and most of the other music had been composed before Beethoven left Bonn, and that he could not allow him any more than he was getting already. He or his staff managed to lose the concerto, but the main themes survive.[2] Beethoven had also written a violin concerto in C before he left Bonn, though he may have achieved no more than the first movement. Most of this survives.[3] No doubt Beethoven wrote both these concertos because he was asked to do so by members of the Elector's orchestra in Bonn.

1 The music has been reconstructed by Willy Hess, and there is an Eulenburg miniature score of his version. The first modern performance was in 1943 with Edwin Fischer as soloist.
2 They are printed in A. W. Thayer, *Life of Beethoven* (revised and edited by Elliot Forbes) (Princeton, 1964), i, p. 126.
3 Printed in Ludwig Schiedermair, *Der junge Beethoven* (Leipzig, 1925), pp. 427–78.

In early maturity Beethoven wrote more piano concertos than symphonies, and like Mozart he might have continued this preference to the end but for his deafness. The three that are now to be discussed have many characteristics in common. Perhaps the most interesting is the way Beethoven unconsciously chooses the same rhythm when he wants a tenderly feminine theme. Three of the four examples quoted below are second subjects, and it will be noticed that *d* is virtually an amalgam of *b* and *a*.

Ex. 1

a) Op. 19

b) Op. 15

c) Op. 15
Largo

d) Op. 37

A minim followed by four quavers may seem so usual as hardly to deserve comment, but in fact the rhythm does not occur as a positive theme either in Beethoven's early piano sonatas or in his first two symphonies, nor for that matter does it occur in the six symphonies Haydn composed in London during his first visit.

CONCERTO NO. 2 IN B FLAT, OP. 19

When Haydn returned from London in the late summer of 1792, he may well have shown Beethoven the six symphonies, nos. 93–98, that he had written there; if so Beethoven would have studied them with interest and profit. It was during Haydn's next trip to England that Beethoven wrote the first of his completed piano concertos, the one in B flat known as no. 2, Op. 19. (Because it was not published until 1801, it acquired a misleading number and opus number; it dates from about the time of the Op. 2 piano sonatas.) Beethoven played it at a concert in March 1795, and again three years later in Prague, for which occasion he rewrote a good deal of it. He later described it, truthfully, as 'not among my best compositions', but for all that it is full of interest.

When Haydn and Beethoven next met they quarrelled, and thereafter Beethoven was at pains to avoid being influenced by his master, but he had no reason to do so when he composed the B flat Concerto, and it is arguably the most Haydnesque work he ever wrote. Even the scoring may show Haydn's influence, for this is Beethoven's only major orchestral work without clarinets, and up to this time Haydn had been curiously averse to these instruments. Beethoven may also have been looking at Mozart's last piano concerto, K.595, which is in the same key and scored for the same band. Mozart nearly always included trumpets and drums in his mature piano concertos but he did not do so in this one, nor did Beethoven in his Op. 19. Both first movements present contrasting ideas inside the first subject; Beethoven began as follows:

Ex. 2

The first bar looks like the start of a Haydn slow introduction, but the tempo is fairly fast. Beethoven had learnt from Mozart to look ahead when devising his main theme; if this can be based on the notes of the common chord it will the more easily fit figuration passages in the development section. Beethoven's falling arpeggio proves as useful as Mozart's rising one, and the former has the advantage of a distinctive rhythm. Beethoven also derived a great deal of music from the marked phrase in his third bar. This is carefully placed so that it will register on the listener's mind, and its development is therefore quite easy to follow, though it may take several hearings before the relevance of the following sequence can be appreciated:

Ex. 3

But the listener is unlikely ever to pick up the following (in bar 23) because the composer himself treats it as insignificant:

Ex. 4

Beethoven was, I suspect, the first composer to look back at what he had written in search of some unconsidered trifle he could build on. He usually foresaw from the start that a theme would have possibilities later (e.g. Ex. 2) and in such cases he 'planted' it carefully. But there were occasions when he scribbled down a series of notes in some transitional passage and realised their possibilities only afterwards (e.g. Ex. 4). In such cases the phrase he develops has not been planted at all, and only the diligent score-reader is likely to discover its origin.

However, the first movement of the B flat Concerto is in general simple to follow. As soon as Beethoven has established Ex. 2, he gives the strings a sweetly Mozartian phrase that he is not going to allow back until the recapitulation. At bar 39 he shows, for the first time in this Concerto, his lifelong obsession for unexpected key changes:

Ex. 5

He may have borrowed this engaging trick of sidestepping up a semitone from Haydn's Symphony no. 93 (bars 165 ff. in the last movement) or no. 96 (bars 129 ff. in the first movement). Then, pivoting on this D flat, he quickly levers the music back through B flat *minor* into the tonic, B flat *major*. Like Mozart, he introduces the piano with a few bars of new and improvisatory music, bars he will repeat when the piano returns for the development section. Also like Mozart he keeps back his most likeable second subject for the piano exposition (Ex. 1a), and even when the material has been heard before, he freshens it with his favourite device of suddenly slipping down to the key a major third below (bar 149) or with a display of pianistic energy; the passage after bar 161 sounds so mature that it probably dates from the 1798 revision.

The slow movement begins with what is virtually Haydn's 'Agnus Dei' rhythm – that is, the first two bars are of the type Haydn often wrote when setting these words in his Masses. Indeed he sometimes used this rhythm at the start of purely instrumental movements – for instance in the slow movement of Symphony no. 87 which Beethoven may not have known, and in the slow movement of no. 98 which he almost certainly did. It was a convention in Beethoven's day that, when a slow-movement tune came round again later on, the soloist elaborated it by adding decorative runs and flourishes of his own devising. This worked well enough when the composer himself was playing the solo part, but it often worked very badly when he was not. In the slow movement of the B flat Concerto Beethoven was at pains to prevent other pianists from ruining the music by writing down his own decorations when the main theme returns (bar 37), and they were so elaborate that nobody since can have seriously thought of adding anything more. Towards the end Beethoven landed his orchestra on the 6/4 chord that conventionally invited a cadenza, but then wrote into the score what might be called an anti-cadenza. Instead of displaying his technique, the pianist has to play, 'con gran espressione', a single line of very slow notes of total simplicity. This is seldom quite convincing in performance, but the idea behind it is original. Nevertheless it cannot be pretended that the *adagio* is one of Beethoven's more interesting slow movements.

The final rondo has a cheerful tune in an unusual rhythm. This perhaps was evolved during the 1798 revision, for the rather tame version in bar 262 looks as though it had been left unaltered by mistake. The sketch-books show that the rondo theme was originally to have been in the 'tame' rhythm throughout.

Ex. 6

Beethoven may have got the rhythm of bar 1 from the Mozart Concerto, K.595 (third movement, bars 198 ff.), and it gives the whole movement piquancy. The main contrasting episode is highly original, for the charming theme ends in a key other than that in which it started. This was to become a favourite device, and it never fails; indeed the main scherzo theme in the Seventh Symphony adopts precisely the same key-change from F major to A major as this Concerto theme. Towards the end (bars 299 ff.) Beethoven anticipated with extreme good humour a tune he was going to write later in the *Pastoral* Symphony (slow movement, bars 13–15).

Just before he began this Concerto Beethoven wrote another rondo in

B flat for piano and orchestra, which may at one time have been intended as the finale.

About 1808 Beethoven realised that he would have to leave the playing of his piano concertos to his pupils, so he wrote cadenzas for them. They are all in the more mature style of his so-called 'middle period', a style that hardly accords with that of the B flat Concerto. Nevertheless pianists are happy to play Beethoven's cadenza for the first movement of the B flat because it is as fine as any ever written by anyone. It begins with a fugato derived from the first bar and a half of the movement (Ex. 2); the dotted rhythm is the same but the arpeggio figure rises instead of falling. Other themes from the first movement are introduced later, and the power of the piano-writing is extraordinary. After such music the six immature bars for orchestra that conclude the movement sound quite meaningless.

CONCERTO NO. 1 IN C, OP. 15

The other piano concerto that Beethoven played in Prague in 1798 was published almost immediately as no. 1 in C, Op. 15, though it had been written three years later than the B flat. It is a longer and more positive work than its predecessor and a very impressive achievement. As in all the early concertos, Beethoven began with a simple theme that would be easy to develop later:

Ex. 7

The octave leap and the dactylic rhythm make this easy to recognise, but in itself it is not very interesting. Beethoven tries to give it as much impact as possible by starting very quietly; an audience will usually pay more attention to a soft beginning than a loud one. There is a precision in what follows that proves characteristic of the whole movement, but in his later concertos Beethoven came to prefer a main theme that had more internal variety, that was beautiful, as well as useful in development.

As in all the early concertos, Beethoven flirts with the notion of changing key for the second subject in his orchestral exposition; the build-up suggests it will come in the tonic, but instead it surprises by being in E flat. Beethoven sees that he must not establish so unconventional a key at this point, and after a mere four bars he interrupts himself with woodwind chords that lift the music up a tone into F minor:

Ex. 8

Again he starts his second subject, and again he manages only four bars of it, after which the woodwind perform the same hoisting action as before. (We shall find Beethoven using exactly the same chords in his *Coriolan* Overture when he wants to repeat his second subject a tone higher.) He continues his orchestral exposition by artfully amalgamating his main themes; the octave leap of the first leads into the descending scale of the second, and the result can be worked in canon. Finally there is a theme that must have been devised specially for the horns and trumpets, and this is even more military in effect than the very precise first subject.

As in the B flat Concerto, the pianist gets his hand in with a few gently irrelevant bars, and these lead predictably into the second exposition. When the second subject turns up in the dominant we realise that previously we were allowed no more than a hint of it; now that there is no need for it to change key, it has space in which to blossom into something shapely and memorable, and its gentle lyricism is the more welcome because of the rather unbending quality of so much music in this movement. In the new key the brass cannot play the military theme, so Beethoven gives it to the woodwind. There is no second subject that occurs in one exposition and not in the other, but the pianist generates energy with some new left-hand triplets of the type also found in the first movement of the *Emperor* Concerto (bar 184):

Ex. 9
a) Op. 15

b) Op. 73

Beethoven often increased the sense of momentum by resorting to triplets. The chromatically shifting passage that comes on the piano a little later must have bewildered the audience in Prague, but it delights today. The usual orchestral tutti has near the end one of those Haydnes-que side-stepping key changes from G to A flat (bars 257 ff.), and then the piano indulges in some rather gentler figuration than is usual in the development section, while the orchestra accompanies unobtrusively with Ex. 7. Beethoven wrote no fewer than three cadenzas for the end of the movement, the third being much the longest and much the best. He twice fools the listener by subsiding on to the sort of trill that conven-tionally ended a cadenza, and then switching to something else. When the cadenza does end, there is no trill at all, but he is careful to provide the best part of a bar's rest so that the pianist has time to bring in the orchestra.

The slow movement is the longest in any Beethoven concerto and its sustained mood of gentle reconciliation is remarkable. As soon as piano and orchestra have shared the main theme (Ex. 1c) the composer, perhaps inadvertently, lets the piano refer to the second subject of the first movement, the rhythm a little changed (bars 18–19). The piano-writing has a gentle lyrical freedom that increasingly suggests a noc-turne as the movement proceeds, and the end is incomparably more 'felt' than it is in the superficially similar slow movement of the B flat.

But as in all the early concertos the final rondo is the most successful movement of the three. The main theme is spirited but loquacious, and it keeps going on when you think it must have ended; Beethoven added the word *scherzando* after his *allegro* tempo mark to show that his intentions were humorous. He took a good deal of this tune from the first movement of an uninteresting piano trio in E flat that he had written in 1791 and never meant to publish. The transformation of this undistinguished music into something irresistible is a small miracle. After a contrasting theme with amiable off-beat accents Beethoven enjoys his favourite trick of suddenly depressing the tonality by a major third. There are fascinating modulations around bar 130, the music sliding up by semitones much as it does in the middle of the 'minuet' of the First Symphony. After the main rondo theme has come round again there is a second episode in the minor key, and this one almost suggests what then passed for 'Turkish' music; good spirits are implicit in every bar. The music goes on and on – there are nearly 600 bars of it – but it is not a bar too long. The movement must have been carefully calculated, but this is not apparent in the exuberant end-product.

CONCERTO NO. 3 IN C MINOR, OP. 37

The C minor Concerto is yet another example of Beethoven achieving a deceptive opus-number by delaying publication. The autograph score is dated 1800 (immediately after the First Symphony and the Op. 18 string quartets) but the Concerto was not performed until April 1803. Beethoven then planned a subscription concert of forbidding length: as well as a repeat performance of the First Symphony and perhaps other works, it included the first performances of his oratorio *The Mount of Olives*, of his Second Symphony, and of his Third Piano Concerto with himself as soloist. The piano part had apparently not been fully written out, and Beethoven played largely from memory. A year later he had to get the notes on paper for a performance by his pupil Ferdinand Ries, who provided the cadenza. Beethoven's own cadenza, usually heard today, was probably not written before 1808.

C minor was as evocative a key for Beethoven as G minor was for Mozart, and many writers have noticed what might be called an emotional resemblance between all Beethoven's C minor works. Often these suggest the frustrated hero, his energy spilling over in defiance. But there is nevertheless an obvious difference between the three periods into which Beethoven's music is conventionally divided, and the C minor Piano Concerto is essentially an early work. It is related not so much to the Fifth Symphony as to the Piano Sonata, Op. 10 no. 1, and the String Quartet, Op. 18 no. 4. There is subdued tension in the quiet opening:

Ex. 10

Bars 3–4 must have been planned from the first with the timpani in mind. In no time he has Ex. 10 in E flat, the relative major of C minor (the usual key contrast in a minor-key work), and he stays there for some 40 bars, by which time he has introduced his second subject (Ex. 1*d*).

The piano is so eager to get at the first subject that three quick, rising scales are sufficient introduction. As in the first movement of the C major, all the themes appear in both expositions, and because the key schemes are similar as well, the expositions are more akin than in most concerto first movements. The piano-writing is rather more difficult than in the previous concertos, but in the development section it becomes curiously restrained. Here the 'timpani' motive is dominant, though it seldom actually occurs on the drums. In the recapitulation Beethoven makes a précis of his first subject, and here at last the lyrical second subject comes in the tonic, where it sounds radiant. It had usually been supposed that after playing a long cadenza soloists would suffer from exhaustion and need a rest while the orchestra ended the movement, but in his C minor Concerto Beethoven keeps the pianist playing right through to the end. I do not know of an earlier instance in a first movement. This is a much longer and more interesting coda than he had previously ventured on, and it was a master-stroke to begin it quietly with the timpani at last making their mark.

The slow movement looks forbidding because Beethoven chose a 3/8 time-signature and thereby landed himself in large quantities of hemidemisemiquavers and worse. Quavers move very slowly indeed, and the mood is one of quiet exaltation. Nothing could be simpler than the form of the movement, which is ternary, and throughout the central section Beethoven broke new ground by making the piano accompany a duet for bassoon and flute with quiet rippling arpeggios. Some pianists find it hard to believe that their music is indeed no more than a background, and when this is the case the bassoon can be very hard to hear. It became a commonplace in romantic concertos for the piano to be given a subsidiary role here and there, but it was very unusual in 1800.

Beethoven had chosen the extraordinary key of E major for his slow movement and the impact of the solo piano at the start can still surprise today. For the rondo finale he had to return to C minor, and he related the movement to its predecessor by devising a theme that emphasised the notes A flat (identical with G sharp) and B natural, two of the three notes in the final chord of the *largo*:

Ex. 11

The mood of this rondo has a certain ambivalence, for there is a latent desperation behind the high spirits; this indeed is partly what makes the main theme so fascinating. After it is over, one senses that Beethoven did not quite know what to do next, but he soon settles on an ebullient new theme for the piano in which the right hand skips down a scale and the left indulges in some mild counterpoint. The third bar of this theme (bar 70) is an echo, presumably unconscious, of the second bar of the main theme. For the second episode Beethoven switches to E flat major and lets the clarinet sing a tune that sounds almost Schubertian. His invention is now at full gallop and presently the main theme becomes a fugue, which gives the music more impetus. When the fugue subsides on to repeated Gs, Beethoven hopes that the informed ear will think this a preparation for a return in C minor. Instead he plays Haydn's ever-successful trick of suddenly stepping up a semitone to A flat (= G sharp), and then switching the piano into the remote key of the slow movement, E major (Ex. 12). We do eventually hear the opening material once more in the home key, but surprise modulations continue almost to the end.

Ex. 12

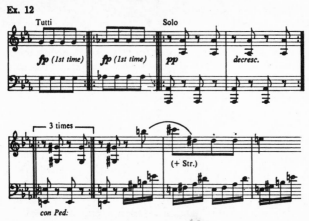

For his coda Beethoven gives way to high spirits and a major key, and has heavily disguised versions of his main themes in 6/8; the resemblance does not extend beyond a bar or two. Beethoven thought his clarinets would find C major a more difficult key than C minor (as indeed they would in those days, though only fractionally), so he left them out of his coda, and the two players have to sit silent and slightly embarrassed in the middle of an industrious and jubilant orchestra.

Concertos with Stringed Instruments

Nothing is known of Beethoven's two Romances for violin and small orchestra other than that both were composed by 1802; but they are so similar in form and oddity that they were probably written at the same time and for the same reason. The form is that of a simple rondo with two episodes; the F major Romance has a more positive coda and also a somewhat higher solo part. The oddity lies in the very existence of these two slow movements. It is just possible that Beethoven wrote them earlier as part of his protracted composition studies, and their general lack of commitment seems to support this suggestion, but it is more likely that he was asked by a violinist friend to compose alternative slow movements for concertos by someone else.

In the winter of 1803–4 Beethoven fell out of love with the traditional slow movement of the kind he had written so often. The concertos that remain to be discussed all have unexpectedly short and simple movements in the middle. And not only the concertos: of the next six piano sonatas in order of composition, three have no slow movement and two have only a brief one. Beethoven turned instead either to the short improvisatory slow movement such as he composed for the *Waldstein* (in place of the original long *andante*) – for two of the late piano sonatas and for the A major Cello Sonata; or (much more often) to some form of variation movement. Both these alternatives saved him from the problem of large-scale construction in slow music, a problem he was perhaps especially disinclined to tackle, as he was now wanting to write much longer first movements than before. Variation form proved endlessly fruitful, giving free rein to his astonishing genius for regenerating a theme, for seeing it from new angles. Sometimes he wrote what, for want of a better word, one might call conventional variations, as in the *Archduke* Piano Trio, in two of the late piano sonatas, and in most of the late string quartets. Sometimes he followed a device of Haydn's and wrote 'double' variations with two themes treated alternately as in the Fifth and Ninth Symphonies and in the A minor Quartet. Sometimes he wrote movements that had elements of variation form as well as contrasting subjects, as in the Seventh Symphony, and it is curious that the 'Andante favori', the movement he cut from the *Waldstein* Sonata, was one of his first experiments in this semi-variation form. He did occasionally revert to the grand-scale conventional slow movement of his younger days, but a change in attitude certainly took place about 1804, and this is especially apparent in the remaining concertos.

CONCERTO IN C, FOR PIANO, VIOLIN AND CELLO, OP. 56

Beethoven wrote most of the Triple Concerto in the astonishing winter of 1803–4, when he managed to compose a whole series of masterpieces. He had more or less finished the *Eroica* by November, by which time he must have begun the Triple Concerto for the then unique combination of piano, violin and cello. The *Eroica* proved a great liberator; in it Beethoven had broken away from the confines of the traditional half-hour symphony, and discovered how to write a first movement with a new spaciousness and in paragraphs of an unprecedented length. He was naturally eager to try out this new style in other instrumental forms, and by the end of the year he had finished the *Waldstein* Sonata and part of the Triple Concerto. In each case the first movement was the longest in its particular category that he had ever attempted, and in each case length became a positive virtue. It is not certain when the Triple Concerto was finished. In January Beethoven interrupted it by starting work on *Fidelio*, and in the spring he had to get the score of the *Eroica* into a finished state. The Triple Concerto may not have been completed for another year or so.

This was the first of a number of works that Beethoven wrote for his young pupil, the Archduke Rudolph, who wanted it for performance by his private orchestra. The Archduke, who was one of the Emperor's sons, was to prove Beethoven's most constant patron; he was a good pianist, and even played the *Emperor* Concerto (which was dedicated to him), and there can be little doubt that he himself took the piano part in the first performance of the Triple Concerto. His violinist was a man named Seidler, his cellist Anton Kraft, who had been Haydn's leading cellist at Esterház; indeed he was at one time credited with the composition of Haydn's best-known cello concerto. It is obvious from Beethoven's score that either the Archduke asked him to give Kraft especial prominence or that he did so on his own account because he so admired Kraft's playing. It is not known when the first performance took place; the first public performance was not given until May 1808.

At the beginning of his symphonies Beethoven usually arrested attention with a loud chord or two, but nearly all his concertos start softly. The Triple Concerto begins with a mere thread of sound on cellos and double basses. The theme is the one on the top stave of Ex. 15, but first sounded an octave lower. Almost at once Beethoven builds it up in an old-fashioned 'Mannheim' crescendo – so called because it was a favourite device of the Mannheim composers in the 1750s; the same note repeated in the bass in quavers was one of its features. An ingratiatingly lovely theme follows this outburst:

Ex. 13

This dissolves into a magical passage:

Ex. 14

This incursion into the remote key of A flat serves no structural purpose – for it ends with Beethoven back where he began – but it achieves to perfection the emotional purpose of pleasurably mystifying the listener. This passage leads into yet another theme in dotted rhythm that might have come out of the Fourth Piano Concerto. Then, with the orchestral exposition drawing to its close, Beethoven gives us eight bars of conventional tonic-and-dominant thumps when four would have been more than enough. However, the disappointment is only momentary.

As in the later movements the cello is the first of the solo instruments to be heard, and the minuscule discords with which it is accompanied are supremely satisfying:

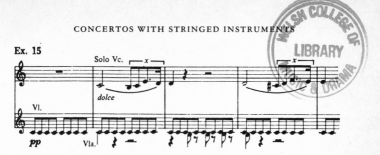

Ex. 15

This is the main theme of the movement, and when it is the piano's turn for it the cellist grumbles along playing on his bottom string what pianists know as an 'Alberti' bass in semiquavers; it is quite ineffectual, and Kraft should have asked Beethoven to think of something better. But in the main the soloists' exposition is magnificent, the themes expansively broad, the tonal scheme splendidly unconventional. Beethoven has been keeping back one of his best tunes for the solo cellist, who sings it gloriously high on the top string, unconcerned that it should still be in the tonic. Beethoven never makes the expected modulation into the dominant. Instead he prefers the more striking contrast of A major for his second-subject group, and this allows him to have Ex. 13 a tone higher than at first with compelling effect. The soloists end their exposition with eight bars of trills which look dull on paper but are very effective in performance; they lead into a somewhat conventional tutti.

Much of the development that follows sounds like chamber music for piano trio, and it is none the worse for that, but there is a miscalculation in the accompanying statements for woodwind. These consist of the phrase *x* in Ex. 15, and because it leads up to nothing on the first beat of the next bar it cannot be played with any effect. Beethoven ends his development with a pleasant tune (bars 299 ff.) that he had written already in the Third Piano Concerto (first movement, bars 36 ff.). There cannot easily be a cadenza with three soloists taking part, and no doubt Beethoven was happy to do without one.

With the *Waldstein* Sonata fresh in his mind, Beethoven followed his seventeen-minute first movement with a slow one lasting only five, and it is perfect. An exquisite theme for the solo cello is followed by a variation set going by the woodwind but played in the main by the solo violin with cello support; throughout this variation the piano contributes a quietly rippling accompaniment. The coda leads without a break into the finale, which is marked *rondo alla polacca*.

The polonaise had been well known as a dance to Bach and his sons, for the Polish court was then at Dresden, the King being also the Elector of Saxony, but in the 1790s its popularity became widespread all over Europe. It was ceremonial and festive, and its individuality lay in the combination of energetic movement with three slow beats to a bar. However, in Beethoven's Triple Concerto the main theme seems to respond better to a lyrical than an energetic approach. As usual the second rondo episode is in the minor, and here the movement anticipates the mood of the noble polonaises Chopin was to write for the piano soon after Beethoven's death:

Ex. 16

This section is splendidly effective. Beethoven leads back to his main theme by way of yet another reminiscence of the Third Piano Concerto (cf. bars 203 ff. with the finale). The end of the movement was too casually written: it may well be that Beethoven, absorbed in *Fidelio*, had lost interest in the work when the Archduke insisted it was finished. The coda (bars 333 ff.) quite lacks the quality of what has gone before. Nevertheless this Concerto rewards attention most generously.

VIOLIN CONCERTO IN D, OP. 61

In the Triple Concerto Beethoven had shown more affection for the solo cello than for the solo violin, but he made ample amends a year or two later in his Violin Concerto in D major. This may not be quite so noble a work in conception as the Triple Concerto, but it is virtually flawless in spite of its rapid composition. Beethoven only just got it finished in time for its first performance on 23 December 1806: he had been writing the Fourth Symphony at the same time and sketching the Fifth. The violinist was Franz Clement, the 26-year-old leader of the band at the Theater an der Wien who had recently directed the first performance of the *Eroica*; Beethoven had known him since he was a boy. Though this is hard to believe, Clement is said to have played much of the solo part in public without any rehearsal, the music not having been written in time. The autograph is full of alterations to the solo part, many of which appear to have been made after the first performance when Clement had had time to make comments.

There are two obvious differences between a concerto for violin and one for piano. First the violin's ability to provide its own harmony is so limited that it cannot normally be given tunes without orchestral accompaniment. Secondly it is much less able than the piano to compete with the orchestra in volume. Accompaniments, even string accompaniments, must be lightly written, except perhaps when the solo part is very high. It follows that violin concertos are likely to be less dramatic than piano concertos, and to suggest agreement rather than conflict between soloist and orchestra. Beethoven's even suggests in the opening movement some measure of agreement between the main themes.

The Concerto begins with five repeated crotchets on the timpani and a tune on the woodwind.

Ex. 17

29

This is a much more melodious start than Beethoven had tried before in his concertos, and it does not matter that the gentle woodwind theme is not obviously suited to development, for the timpani crotchets provide a rhythmic cell that will fit almost anything; in fact this rhythmic cell draws the whole movement into a unity. In bar 10 Beethoven presents it on D sharp, which relates neither to what has gone before nor to what comes after; this is his way of making sure that it registers. We hear the rhythmic cell again under the second subject:

Ex. 18

The divine simplicity of this theme is beyond praise. Beethoven relates it to the almost equally feminine first subject by building it on the rhythm first heard in bar 8. Although the lack of contrast between the two subjects is partly due to the solo violin's unsuitability in stern masculine music, Beethoven has, in fact, been showing less and less interest in this particular contrast for some time; the different themes are much more in agreement in the Triple Concerto and the Fourth Piano Concerto than they are in the earlier concertos, when thematic contrasts are usually extreme. Almost at once he repeats Ex. 18 in the minor key; the device was to be much used by Schubert. At the end of the orchestral exposition there is yet a third theme in much the same rhythm, its two-bar phrases alternating on the violins and low down on cellos and double basses.

The soloist is brought in with a few improvisatory bars and the music soon rises celestially so that the violin can sing the first subject at the very top of its compass. This is often done in later violin concertos but it is hard to think of an earlier example of a tune that seems especially invented for such a purpose. No new themes are necessary in the violin's exposition, for Beethoven's resource in composing figuration passages is endless. The expected tutti at the end is prepared for as though it were to be in the usual dominant key, A major, but at the very last moment Beethoven slips into F major – precisely what he had done at the same point in the Triple Concerto. In both works a good deal of what follows is a mere repetition in a new key of music that has been heard earlier; in the Violin Concerto he repeats his second-subject group very much as it was in the orchestral exposition. In the development section orchestral interjections below the violin part alternate between the five repeated crotchets and the almost circular theme in bars 4–5 of Ex. 17 which comes in thirds; sometimes he has it in quavers at double speed. From bar 330 the repeated crotchets occur on the horns for a remarkable passage in G minor:

Ex. 19

The solo violin writing is here at its most romantic and poignant; consequently it has become a tradition for the tempo to drop suddenly to andante, though no change can have been wanted by Beethoven or he would have marked one. The tradition probably goes back to Joachim, the violinist who first made this Concerto popular. The first violinist to record it, Kreisler, used to drop from 112 crotchets a minute to 66, a more extreme change than is usual today when the G minor passage is generally taken at about 80. It would be interesting to hear it played as written. The return to the composer's tempo is always made during the passage over a pedal A leading to the recapitulation. This begins with the first subject played fortissimo by the full orchestra; it was unusual for Beethoven to transform a theme in this Lisztian way. No cadenza survives earlier than Joachim's, but Kreisler's is preferred by most violinists. As in the Third Piano Concerto Beethoven keeps the soloist playing to the end of the movement, the second and third themes being treated with a magical simplicity and calm. The almost hypnotic effect is carried over into the next movement.

The slow movement is usually taken rather more slowly than the *larghetto* marking would seem to imply, but it may perhaps be more effective our way than Beethoven's. This is one of his semi-variation movements. There is virtually no attempt at contrast, and no change of key. The music sustains throughout the same mood of absolute still-ness. There are two themes, and the solo violin plays only the second of them in its simple form.

Theme A   Muted strings

    Var. 1   Theme on horns, then on clarinet. The violin accom-
                 panies divinely in this and the next variation

Var. 2	Theme on the bassoon
Var. 3	The orchestra alone, fairly loud
Theme B	Solo violin
Var. 4	Theme on solo violin, decorated
Theme B	Solo violin, decorated
Coda	

Beethoven asks the soloist to link this movement to the finale with a short cadenza. As Menuhin once pointed out in a letter to *The Times*, Kreisler made the mistake here of anticipating the theme of the finale and thereby spoilt its impact; Joachim on the other hand made a superfluous return to the main slow movement theme. 'I merely shelter behind Beethoven's own suggestion of "cadenza *ad libitum*" and simply play an arpeggio to bridge the two openings as two octaves apart, omitting all further musical comment as redundant.'

The final rondo is so famous and so simple that few words are necessary. By having his main theme note-for-note the same each time it occurs, Beethoven saved himself the trouble of writing it down more than once, leaving the rest to his copyist. As usual the second episode is in the minor (bars 127 ff.), and the violin's new tune is agreeably repeated by the bassoon. At least the effect is agreeable if the solo violin keeps its accompanying semiquavers quiet enough for the bassoon to be audible. This is one of the very few occasions when Beethoven's music seems to anticipate that of Mendelssohn. After what one always hopes will be a brief cadenza, he indulges in a magical key-change, with the rondo theme suddenly appearing in A flat (bars 292 ff.). He gets back to the tonic by means of four dotted minims played unaccompanied by the solo violin, and their resemblance to the third bar of the slow movement is presumably unintentional. The perfectly timed surprise-ending of this movement never ceases to satisfy.

In the spring of 1807 Clementi was in Vienna hoping to buy the English rights in some of Beethoven's works; he had recently set up in London as a music publisher. He was especially impressed by the beauty of the Violin Concerto, and because he thought there would be very few performances of it in England he asked Beethoven to rewrite it as a piano concerto. This was a more sensible commission than it may seem at first sight; there were in fact very few performances of the work anywhere in its original form until Joachim took it up in the 1840s. Beethoven did not alter the orchestration, and took only a minimum of trouble over rewriting the solo part. He did, however, invent some new accompaniment figures for the pianist's left hand, as for instance in the main rondo theme, and he composed a highly original cadenza for the first movement with the timpani joining in throughout with the five repeated crotchets. Max Rostal has adapted this piano cadenza for the violin, preserving the interesting timpani part. The result must be a good deal closer to what Beethoven might have liked than anything written years later by Joachim or Kreisler, but violinists are a conservative breed and they have not so far shown much interest in it.

Clementi was very slow in publishing the Violin Concerto, but, as Alan Tyson has shown,[1] he acquired efficiency with time and managed to bring out all Beethoven's music from Op. 73 to Op. 83 before anyone on the Continent. Thus the very first publication anywhere of two works discussed in the next section, the Choral Fantasia and the *Emperor* Concerto, was by Clementi's firm in London.

---

[1] *The Authentic English Editions of Beethoven* (London, 1963), p. 52.

The Later Piano Concertos

CONCERTO NO. 4 IN G, OP. 58

It has been convenient to delay consideration of the G major Fourth Piano Concerto until this point, even though it was finished in March 1806 shortly before the Violin Concerto was begun. We have seen Beethoven contriving simple themes with which to begin his piano concertos so that he might have something suitable for development later on, and we have seen that in one instance the resulting theme was of no great musical interest in itself. By 1806 he had evolved a wonderfully simple solution to the problem: he searched for a subject of real quality, one that had both melodic interest and rhythmic variety, and anchored it in some way to an extremely simple rhythmic cell consisting of repeated notes. He did this at the start of the Violin Concerto, and he began his Fourth Piano Concerto and Fifth Symphony in very similar fashion. Indeed the rhythmic cell in the last-named works is virtually the same:

Ex. 20

But though the repeated-note rhythm is so similar the effect is utterly different, and it is easy to see that a composer obsessed with the problems of varying a theme would be equally stimulated by the problem of writing two major first movements on the same rhythm and contriving that they should be poles apart emotionally. The start of the Fourth Piano Concerto 'feels' different from the start of the Fifth Symphony because of its major key, its gentler tempo, its less aggressive scoring, and the way the rhythm is embedded in common-chord harmonies. It is a remarkable start in a number of ways. Only Mozart had previously allowed the piano to join in the opening bars (in his E flat

34

Concerto, K.271), but he had done so with much less striking effect. The quietness of the piano opening was predictable, for Beethoven usually began his concertos unobtrusively, but no one could have foreseen the five-bar phrase with its extraordinary rhythmic variety, or the orchestral entry in B major. Throughout the orchestral exposition that follows, the four repeated quavers are gently emphasised by instrument after instrument, and we can soon sense that Beethoven is creating a quite individual mood from which he will scarcely deviate throughout the Concerto. This is surely the most poetic of the piano concertos and the least aggressive, the music being infused with a universal benevolence.

It would hardly be possible not to be captivated by Beethoven's second subject, the enchanting originality of which derives from its incessant change of key:

Ex. 21

Though this is not apparent in the quotation, the A minor start was itself something of a jerk, so for the first four bars Beethoven confines himself to a conventional modulation. He then prods the tonality into C for a repeat of his engaging four-bar phrase, and by deft alteration contrives that it shall now end a semitone below the start in B minor. Fascinated by this conjuring trick he does it again, this time slipping from G major to F sharp minor. In the course of twelve bars the theme has ventured on six different keys.

The piano re-entry is so ambiguous that one has the impression the player does not quite know what key the Concerto is in, but he soon settles down. There is a new theme in this second exposition, and it will be no surprise that it begins conventionally in D, the dominant of G, and ends after four bars in B minor:

Ex. 22

The third bar of this is in the same rhythm as the third bar of Ex. 20*b*, and it has a sforzando in the same place. When these four bars are repeated, the piano provides piquant discords on every beat. Though this movement never sounds especially fast, Beethoven's frequent use of triplet semiquavers in the solo part demands some of the most rapid note-playing in any concerto; the solo part is even more difficult than it sounds. Beethoven took full advantage of the new notes that manufacturers had recently added at the top of the piano keyboard.

At the end of the soloist's exposition Beethoven misleads his listeners with four bars of trills that seem to promise the usual tutti, but in fact the tutti comes when it is *not* expected – after a languishingly beautiful tune on the piano that does not seem to be leading up to anything. The development section presents some problems of balance; there is so much going on that the first-subject rhythm on the woodwind is often hard to hear. Beethoven shows astonishing resource in contriving piano figuration that is emotive as well as decorative. As in the Violin Concerto he dares to start his recapitulation with the gentle opening theme played fortissimo – by the piano. The addition of very high, soft piano-writing, above the orchestra's B major entry, is entrancing. The cadenza he wrote for this movement is not among his best, though it is more suitable than most of those written by others: the one by Brahms manages to make all the themes sound as though Brahms himself had composed them. As in all the later concertos, Beethoven keeps his soloist quietly busy after the cadenza until the end of the movement.

It seems that Liszt was the first to suggest a programmatic basis for the slow movement, and indeed it must be obvious to any listener that the piano is having a discussion with the strings and trying to soothe them. They play alternately; the piano is never allowed the disturbed string-theme and the strings are never allowed the piano's soothing one. By the end of this short movement the piano has clearly won the strings over to its point of view. As E. M. Forster put it in a 1935 essay, 'Wordmaking and Sound-taking':

> It is very easy music; it strikes or strokes immediately, and elderly gentlemen before myself have called it 'Beauty and the Beast'. What about Orpheus and the Furies, though? . . . When the movement begins I always repair to the entrance of Hell and descend under the guidance of Gluck through diminishing opposition to the Elysian Fields. . . . The piano turns into Orpheus and the strings, waving less and less their snaky locks, sink at last into acquiescence with true love.

The finale is tonally linked to the *andante* with precisely the same device as at the same point in the C minor Concerto. The slow movement has ended with a chord of E minor, so Beethoven begins the *vivace* with a chord having two notes – E and G – in common with it: C major. The theme is then in the wrong key and only works round to the right one, G major, some eight or ten bars later. Haydn had sometimes begun themes in the wrong key, for instance at the start of the first *allegro* in the *Surprise* Symphony, but with him the jerk is only momentary; Beethoven goes on for several bars. At much the same time as he wrote this movement he was planning the second *Razumovsky* String Quartet, where he began the finale in the same way. The half-humorous cadence at the end of this Concerto theme owes something to the finale theme in Mozart's B flat String Quartet, K.458.

Like all Beethoven's concerto finales, this one is a rondo. The main contrasting subject has a curious touch of perversity, with its remote feeling and rather halting rhythm, but when it is played at the end of the movement by the cellos and violins in canon (bars 475 ff.), it acquires unexpected warmth. There is an even more striking transformation of the main theme, which becomes romantic rather than humorous when played legato by three solo strings (two violas and one cello) below figuration triplets high on the piano (bars 366 ff.; see also bars 520 ff.). By now Beethoven is so resourceful that he no longer needs two episodes in his rondos as in the past; both this finale and the one in the *Emperor* Concerto manage with only one.

FANTASIA IN C MAJOR, OP. 80, FOR PIANO, ORCHESTRA AND CHORUS

On 22 December 1808 Beethoven gave what proved to be the last subscription concert in which he himself performed. Its main purpose was to introduce to the public his Fifth and Sixth Symphonies. A few days before, the newspapers advertised a last-minute addition: 'A Fantasia for the Pianoforte which ends with the gradual entrance of the entire orchestra and the introduction of choruses as a finale.' Both on this occasion and during a charity concert the previous month Beethoven got at loggerheads with his orchestra, and in the Choral Fantasia there was a complete breakdown which the players thought was his fault. Because he realised that his increasing deafness was to blame, he never again played a concerto in public.

The Fantasia was not a choral work with a piano part. As the advertisement reveals, Beethoven saw it as a piano concerto with two entirely new features – the addition of a chorus being only one of them. Later on he planned an overture with chorus parts, and later still he brought the chorus into his last symphony. In oratorios, Masses and operas the orchestra was subservient to the voices; Beethoven was exercised by the quite new idea of writing music in which the voices were subservient to the instruments.

The Fantasia was among the very few works Beethoven wrote without any interruption, and its failings are mainly due to haste. But these are more than offset by the extraordinary originality of the conception. Instead of a three-movement concerto, he planned a long single movement based on his semi-variation form, and in the course of it he managed to foreshadow both Ravel's *Bolero*, in the gradual build-up from small beginnings to an all-embracing fortissimo, and Britten's *Variations on a Theme of Purcell* in the way the orchestral instruments are introduced one by one. He began with an improvisation for piano alone; what we have today was written only after the performance. In fact, the impressive C minor start may have been distantly influenced by the beginning of Mozart's equally improvised Fantasia in D minor. This opening piano solo has not found much favour with scholars and critics, but it has a good deal of power and holds the interest with ease.

After three or four minutes Beethoven instructs the soloist to bring in the orchestra. Because he wants to build up a long climax, he starts with some very quiet music in which nothing seems to be happening; but eventually the piano is given what is virtually the only theme in the entire twenty-minute work. Beethoven took it from an early song of about 1795, a setting of Bürger's 'Gegenliebe',[1] and we with our hindsight of the choral theme in the Ninth Symphony can see that he must have been obsessed for most of his life with the search for a totally simple melody that abjured all rhythmic variety and striking leaps, a melody that moved in notes of equal length and rose or fell by intervals of no more than a tone. Here is the first half of the one in the Fantasia:

Ex. 23

1 Since Bürger's words were unsuitable for the Fantasia, a fresh text had to be written – possibly by Christoph Kuffner, who did not, however, include it in his collected works.

The horns have helped to prepare for this theme, and they stay to accompany its presentation on the piano. Then follow five very simple variations in which other instruments are introduced with a clarity that seems almost to have an educational purpose. I have numbered the variations, but they were not numbered by Beethoven:

Var. 1: The flute decorates the theme; the piano accompanies.
Var. 2: The oboes decorate the theme; the piano accompanies.
Var. 3: Two clarinets and bassoon on their own.
Var. 4: String quartet.
Var. 5: Full orchestra (for the first time in the work).

After a short interlude that ends in a very brief written-out cadenza, there follow three long and very free variations of considerable complexity:

Var. 6: This begins in Beethoven's stormy C minor vein, and then surprises by slipping into B major for an enchanting pianissimo passage in three-bar rhythm.
Var. 7: An *adagio* in A major. The piano has a highly decorated version of the theme, and the accompaniment alternates between woodwind and lower strings (two violas and a cello).
Var. 8: A military march in F. This subsides into some of the finest music in the work, the piano modulating freely in Beethoven's best manner.

There is a brief cadenza, and a brief return to the negative music heard when the orchestra first came in, and Beethoven then plays his trump card, the chorus. The singers dominate in the three very simple variations that follow:

Var. 9: Three women soloists, accompanied only by the piano.
Var. 10: Three male soloists, accompanied by piano and pizzicato strings.
Var. 11: Full chorus and orchestra, suddenly loud.

The 'interlude' music returns and leads into a long *presto* coda in which the piano proves something of an embarrassment. The chorus is twice given a splendid climax with two wonderful key changes – Ex. 24 overleaf. The orchestra plays the same harmonies mainly in repeated quavers. Beethoven liked the effect so well that he repeated it in the finale of the Ninth Symphony (bars 640–6) with slight but significant changes.

For a number of reasons the Fantasia is not often performed today. Because there are less than five minutes of choral writing, it is not interesting to choral societies; because pianists do not expect to find a chorus taking part in orchestral concerts, they seldom include the work

Ex. 24
(Presto)

wenn sich Lieb' und Kraft, und Kraft,

und Kraft

in their repertoire. No one claims it as a masterpiece, and some have suggested that it is hardly worth performing. But if Beethoven has your sympathy, you can hardly fail to be interested in so extraordinary and original a conception, whatever its weaknesses.

CONCERTO NO. 5 IN E FLAT (*EMPEROR*), OP. 73 *1809*

Beethoven began his fifth and last piano concerto immediately after the Fantasia, so he may not at first have reconciled himself to the idea that his piano-playing days were over. But it was not publicly performed until 11 February 1812, three years after its completion, and the delay was probably due to the composer's reluctance to undertake the solo part himself. When at last his pupil Carl Czerny played it, the audience was not enthusiastic. In the eighteen years that remained to him Beethoven wrote no more concertos, though he continued to compose in all his other favourite forms.

The Fifth Piano Concerto is the most spectacular of the five, and in Britain it is known as the *Emperor*. The key is E flat, so often the one Beethoven chose for his noblest thoughts, and the first movement is an enormous piece of invention, much longer in both pages and time than the other two movements put together. He managed to find for it yet another original opening – a grand cadenza for the piano punctuated by three massive chords on the orchestra. When at last he comes to the orchestral exposition, he begins it with the most positive theme in any of his concertos, and only later does he reveal that it is artfully compounded of three rhythmic or melodic units suitable for development:

Ex. 25

As in the first movement of the Violin Concerto, the second subject is presented in both the major and the minor, but the juxtaposition in the *Emperor* is much more sophisticated. The major version is limited to notes playable on the horns for which it must have been specially designed, but it is the minor version that comes first:

Ex. 26
a)

b)

This is, as it were, a surprise modulation, not of key but of mood, and considering that the notes are virtually the same the difference in effect is extraordinary.

Beethoven brings in the piano a little earlier than might be expected over the orchestra's build-up in the dominant. Mozart had done much the same in the first movement of his C major Concerto, K.467. The piano treats the first subject in compulsive fortissimo, and one is reminded of the recapitulation in the first movement of the Fourth Piano Concerto. Even more remarkable is the superb flood of invention with which Beethoven adapts the second subject to the new conditions of piano-domination. It may have been conceived as a horn theme, but the fact that, in this key, the horns cannot play it only stimulated him to new flights of fancy. With mesmeric effect the piano has the minor version in the extraordinary key of B minor; for the repeat in the major, Beethoven slides into the conventional dominant, B flat, and has the whole orchestra thumping it out in aggressive semi-staccato. The variety of moods this theme can convey is without limit. As so often, the exposition ends with echoes of the first subject, and the piano generates energy with the triplets quoted in Ex. 9b; it will be noticed that these triplets underpin a phrase from the first subject.

The tutti that follows is unusually conventional in that it begins with the first subject in the dominant, and the development is also conventional since the woodwind quietly murmur fragments of the first subject against difficult piano figuration – but 'conventional' is a misleading word for such Olympian music. Beethoven prefaces his recapitulation with a cut version of the opening cadenza, and then repeats the exposition material with some striking changes. The piano has the quiet, mysterious minor-key version of the second subject in the wonderfully remote key of C sharp minor, and when Beethoven wrenches the tonality back to the tonic for the repeat in the major, he ignores the fact that he originally thought of this as a horn theme, and once again has the whole orchestra thumping it out aggressively. (This is, indeed, one of his most aggressive movements.) A tutti seems to be leading up to an extemporised cadenza, but Beethoven feels he has pandered enough to the pianist's exhibitionist cravings, and for the third time in the movement he writes down what must be played. The result is so short and so restrained that it hardly ranks as a cadenza. Beethoven's chief aim is to treat his second subject as it deserves, and in no time the piano has the mysterious version in the correct key, E flat minor, and this leads to a return of the orchestra which manages to be both utterly natural and utterly unexpected. Heralded by no trills, the horns suddenly play their own major version of the theme; it is more than a quarter of an hour since we last heard it as it should be – legato and celestially calm. This is much the longest coda in any concerto movement by Beethoven, and it ends with a splendid display of energy.

As in all the later concertos the slow movement is brief, and as in all but one it has elements of variation form. The key, B major, is not as unconventional as it looks. B major is the same as C flat major, and thus a major third below the key of the first movement; the slow movement of the C major Concerto showed exactly the same relationship. Muted strings sing a simple theme of two four-bar phrases followed by a two-bar phrase that comes twice. The mood is peaceful and static – just what is needed between outer movements of titanic energy and drive. The piano rhapsodises briefly and then plays the first of two variations on the theme heard at the start; in the second the woodwind have the melody and the piano accompanies. A short coda leads into the finale, with the piano hinting in very slow notes at the rumbustious music to come.

Like the first movement, the rondo has a main theme of enormous power with a very great deal of internal variety. Its start is so syncopated that we cannot at first detect what the true time-signature is. One of its later elements suggests galloping, and this rhythm is stressed by the orchestra in an extension of the first subject. As in the finale of the Fourth Concerto Beethoven manages with only one contrasting episode, and this is so overshadowed by the main theme that in retrospect it is hard to recall how it goes. It is something of a surprise to discover that it comes both times in the tonic, E flat, the second time as part of a note-for-note repeat of all the opening material.

The device left him with the problem of providing key-variety elsewhere, and he solved it triumphantly in a splendid development section. Three times the piano starts to play the main theme and each time is quickly distracted into jubilant display. These false starts occur in C major, A flat and E major; thus each is a major third below its predecessor. The principal return of the main tune is introduced with an echo of the final bars from the slow movement. The coda is distinguished by a quietly impressive passage in which the piano is accompanied only by the galloping rhythm on the timpani.

The Classical Overture

By the beginning of the nineteenth century, when Beethoven wrote his earliest overtures, the old three-movement type practically identical (and sometimes actually identical) with the concert symphony had become obsolete. But the one-movement overture was – despite the precedents of Mozart's later overtures – often very tenuously linked with the opera it introduced, and sometimes not linked at all. An overture could be switched from one opera to another without loss of effect, as Rossini was still demonstrating during Beethoven's maturity. Yet the pointlessness of the generalised overture had been noticed even before Handel died. In 1755 the Italian dilettante Count Algarotti published his *Saggio sopra l'opera in musica*, and thirteen years later an anonymous Englishman translated his remarks about opera overtures as follows:

> Among the errors observable in the present system of music, the most obvious, and that which first strikes the ears at the very opening of an opera, is the hackneyed manner of composing overtures, which are always made to consist of two allegro movements with a grave in between and to be as noisy as possible. Thus they are void of variation and so jog on much alike. Yet what a wide difference ought to be perceived between that, for example, which precedes the death of Dido, and that which is prefixed to the nuptials of Demetrius and Cleonice. The main drift of an overture should be to announce, in a certain [i.e. positive] manner, the business of the drama and consequently prepare the audience to receive those affecting impressions that are to result from the whole of the performance.

Much the same point was made by Gluck in the dedication of his opera *Alceste* in 1769, the year before Beethoven was born:

> I have felt that the overture ought to apprise the spectators of the nature of the action that is to be represented and to form, so to speak, its argument.

Gluck tried to put this precept into practice (in ways that are not always very clear to modern audiences), but few other composers were prepared to follow.

Some adopted a more naïve way of linking their overtures to what followed: the practice of introducing tunes that were later to be sung seems to have originated in Parisian operas with spoken dialogue; by 1770 it was becoming quite common in the overtures of Monsigny,

Grétry, and their contemporaries, and it has been followed ever since by composers of operettas and musical comedies throughout the world. But at first the device was felt to be too trivial for Italian operas. In the overture to his German *Singspiel, Die Entführung aus dem Serail*, Mozart quite obviously quoted Belmonte's opening aria, but in *Così fan tutte* the quotation in the overture is such that few in the audience probably noticed it. By 1820 Weber was basing his overtures entirely on themes that were to be heard after the curtain rose, but most of his operas have spoken dialogue. There are hardly any such links in the all-sung Italian operas that Rossini wrote at much the same time. We shall find Beethoven anticipating melodies that were to be sung in his overtures to *Fidelio*, *King Stephen* and *The Ruins of Athens*, but in every case there was spoken dialogue in German.

PROMETHEUS, OP. 43

Beethoven's earliest overture was written for a ballet, *Die Geschöpfe des Prometheus* (The Creatures of Prometheus), first performed at the Vienna Burgtheater on 28 March 1801. The comparatively late opus number is deceptive, for the music was written just after the Op. 18 string quartets. As so often with Beethoven, opus numbers indicate the date of publication, not of composition.

The original playbill told the audience that they would see how two statues, created and given life by Prometheus, were 'through the power of harmony made susceptible to all the passions of human life. Prometheus leads them to Parnassus for instruction by Apollo, god of the arts. Apollo commands Amphion, Arion and Orpheus to acquaint them with music, Melpomene and Thalia with tragedy and comedy, Terpsichore and Pan with the shepherd dance, and Bacchus with the heroic dance.' From the much more detailed scenario in Carlo Ritorni's biography of the author-choreographer, Salvatore Vigano, we learn that at the beginning, 'pursued by the violent anger of heaven, which provides a pretext for a noisy musical prelude, Prometheus comes running through the wood to his two clay statues. . . .' This 'noisy prelude' was not, of course, the overture but an *introduzione* (entitled 'La Tempesta' in some early scores), into which the overture ran without a break; the last four bars of the overture in its usual form are a concert-ending.

The slow introduction begins with a chord whose B flat suggests a move to the subdominant before the tonic, C major, has been established; it was a device Beethoven had used a few months earlier at the start of his First Symphony, which is also in C. The main theme of the *allegro* is a moto perpetuo running non-stop in quavers. As in so many of Beethoven's themes, the first four bars are immediately repeated a tone higher.

The *Prometheus* overture may have been one of the works played by the amateur orchestra that grew out of the Schubert family string quartet, for traces of it occur in two of the early symphonies Schubert composed for this group. The opening of the *adagio* is echoed at the start of Schubert's Sixth Symphony, and the moto perpetuo *allegro* theme that recurs a tone higher at bar 5 was copied at the same structural point in his Second Symphony.

The Opera Overtures

The four overtures Beethoven wrote for his only opera, *Fidelio*, show him struggling with material of the very highest quality that for various reasons proved difficult to handle, and they thus allow us a unique opportunity of studying his mind at work. Anyone who composes four overtures for one opera must be worrying either that he has not attained his object or that he has been mistaken as to what that object should be. At different times Beethoven suffered from both worries. *Leonore II* was written for the original three-act version of *Fidelio*, which failed partly because of the poor libretto and partly because Napoleon's army was occupying Vienna. There were only three performances, the first on 20 November 1805. The overture was not published until 1842, and not published complete until 1853; for a time the coda had been lost. *Leonore III* was written for the unsuccessful two-act revision of the opera, which was now called *Leonore*. There were only two performances, the first of them on 29 March 1806. The overture was published in 1810, and has always been much the most popular of the four in the concert-hall. *Leonore I* was not certainly performed until 1828, just after Beethoven's death, and was not published until ten years later. It is not known why or when he wrote it. *Fidelio* was written for the successful third version of the opera, but only finished in time for the second performance on 26 May 1814. It is this third version of the opera that has almost always been performed, and indeed published, ever since.

The placing of *Leonore I* is conjectural. The evidence one way or the other is uncertain, and we have to rely mainly on psychological probability if we are to decide whether it was written before or after *Leonore II* and *III*. Beethoven's close friend, Anton Schindler, wrote in 1840 that *Leonore I* was the first of these overtures to be composed. 'As soon as it was finished, the composer himself was dissatisfied with it, as were his friends. The piece was played by a small orchestra at Prince Lichnowsky's, and pronounced . . . wanting in ideas, style and character. It was therefore laid aside.' If Schindler were a trustworthy biographer, this testimony would be enough, but his book is notoriously inaccurate; and he had not yet met Beethoven at this period. It would also have been out of character for Beethoven to scrap *Leonore I* at the suggestion of aristocratic friends who had never seen the opera, and could have known very little about it. Nevertheless a number of recent scholars have supported Schindler over this, including Elliot Forbes (the editor and reviser of Thayer's *Life of Beethoven*) and Emily Anderson (the best

translator of Beethoven's letters).[1] On the other hand Ignaz von Sey-
fried, a theatre conductor who published a not altogether reliable book
on Beethoven in 1832, suggested that *Leonore I* was composed after *II*
and *III* for a projected production in Prague in 1807, because Beethoven
thought *Leonore III* would be too difficult for the Prague orchestra. One
other circumstance might account for its later composition. On 4 May
1806, soon after the second version of the opera had been staged,
Beethoven wrote to one of the theatre directors asking for some of the
orchestral parts 'because Prince Lobkowitz is thinking of having a
performance of the opera at his palace'. It is not known if this performance ever took place. If it did, Beethoven may well have written yet
another overture (for reasons we shall come to later), and this may well
have been 'pronounced wanting in ideas, style and character' and laid
aside. (Schindler would not be the only Beethoven expert to confuse
Prince Lobkowitz with Prince Lichnowsky.) The later date for *Leonore I*
has found favour with Thayer, Nottebohm and Tovey, among others.

Fidelio was an 'escape' opera of the type developed in Paris during and
after the French Revolution. Florestan is unjustly held in prison and
about to be executed. His wife, Leonore, disguises herself as a man so
that she can get a job in the prison and thus have an opportunity to save
her husband; she calls herself Fidelio. Beethoven saw the kernel of the
plot in the *adagio* of an aria Florestan sings when in his cell in Act II.

Ex. 27

The words can be roughly translated: 'In the springtime of life happiness
has deserted me. I dared to speak the truth boldly, and fetters are my
reward.' Beethoven attached such importance to this part of the opera
that he sketched as many as eighteen variants of Florestan's melody
(Ex. 27 shows the form sung in the third version of the opera), and used
some of them in his overtures. In *Leonore II* this *adagio* might be
described as the main theme; it is also important in *III*, but much less so
in *I*. Beethoven wanted his overture to express the plight of the prisoner
at the start and the rapture of his rescue at the end. Accordingly he
decided to introduce the two trumpet calls which, in the opera,

---

1   *Letters of Beethoven* (three vols. London, 1961). Later quotations are from this translation.

announce the last-minute arrival of Florestan's reprieve. These would come best just before an ecstatic coda: thus the overture, in Gluck's words, would 'apprise the spectators of the nature of the action'.

LEONORE II, OP. 72

Leonore II begins with a vast slow introduction based almost entirely on Florestan's *adagio*. The uncertainty of the imprisoned man is symbolised by the uncertainty of key; C major is abandoned almost at once as the music slips into a mysterious B minor; Florestan's melody is in A flat and 25 bars elapse before Beethoven gets back to C. Here is the beginning:

Ex. 28

Beethoven may have meant the three descending notes at the start of his overture to anticipate the three descending notes at the start of the *adagio*, but they are not in the same part of the scale and the resemblance may be accidental. (In *Leonore III* it virtually disappears, for Beethoven cut the first two bars.) In this first version of the opera (and of the overture) the *adagio* theme has an additional bar of hesitation between bars 3 and 4 of Ex. 27.

Beethoven reaches the main *allegro* with two of his most astonishing bars:

Ex. 29

For some time the exposition is much the same as it was to be in *Leonore III*; in both overtures the *adagio*, visually disguised in long notes, forms the second subject, and in both it is in the rather unusual key of E major. Soon Beethoven is developing his two main themes with masterly breadth and invention; there is a notable section in which the woodwind chatter apprehensively in one-bar phrases over a sustained repetition of the first-subject rhythm:

Ex. 30

It may well have been at this point that Beethoven realised that what he was planning would be on a much larger scale than any previous overture. There was more than ten minutes of it, and he still had not reached the recapitulation. By the time it was finished it might well play for over fifteen minutes, twice as long as any audience would expect. Whatever his reason, he decided on the extraordinary solution of cutting the recapitulation. At the climax of the development he rushed straight into his trumpet sequence (the reprieve and rescue), allowed a five-bar repeat of the *adagio* (now in C major), and then hurried into the coda. Even then, the result was the longest overture he ever wrote.

In the original version of the opera, the trumpet calls were in B flat. But this was an unsuitable key for an overture in C major at a point when informed ears would be expecting the tonic, and Beethoven preferred E flat; this meant that he had to modify the triplet figuration to keep the calls within the trumpet's compass. The result was a good deal less striking than the strong and simple fanfare he later wrote for *Leonore III*. Indeed the whole episode is a little unsatisfactory, in spite of its blazing originality, for the eight bars that separate the trumpet calls are almost inept; Beethoven seems to be planning a modulation but has to cancel it before it makes any sense. One wonders why he did not write down the marvellous bars that separate the trumpet calls in *Leonore III*, for they were already present in the first version of the opera.

LEONORE III

When *Fidelio* was first staged in 1805 Beethoven cannot have given any thought to the overall suitability of *Leonore II* in its context, but he certainly noticed a number of inadequacies, and when it was decided to revive the opera in the following March he rewrote the overture with extreme care and also with astounding inspiration. There can be no doubt that his main object was to leave room for a recapitulation.

Every music-lover knows that *Leonore III* is one of Beethoven's supreme masterpieces, but he achieved it at the cost of some wonderful music; in some ways *Leonore II* is the grander conception of the two. But if a recapitulation were to be included, much of it would have to be cut. Beethoven reduced the slow introduction by about a minute and a half, and thereby lost the marvellously vacillating repeat of Florestan's *adagio*. He also cut the last two bars of the introduction and odd phrases here and there in the *allegro*. Then, when he came to the E major second subject, he developed a four-note rising scale from *Leonore II* and changed Florestan's *adagio* into something so magically different that one could be forgiven for not at first recognising it.

Ex. 31

He increased tension by tightening a canon at one bar's interval into a canon at half a bar's interval. By now inspiration was flowing so well that he put *Leonore II* right out of his mind, and started developing the rising first subject against a new, falling derivative of the Florestan theme, with memorably piquant clashes on some of the main beats.

Ex. 32

It was sad that there was no room for the development sequence shown in Ex. 30, but he worked something very similar into the coda (bars 480 ff.) of the first movement of his Ninth Symphony.

Beethoven had simplified and strengthened the trumpet call when revising the opera, and *Leonore III* profited from the revision; this time he preserved the magical bars that separate the trumpet calls. He was also able to keep the trumpet's key of B flat. He could not effectively go straight from this to the recapitulation in C, but he did not now need to because he had saved at least three minutes. So he allowed the flute a false recapitulation in G (rapturous birdsong – a symbol of freedom?) and reached his C major with a superb climax of sound. There was still no time to waste, so he got through his first-subject group in 25 bars (as opposed to 83 in the exposition), and took far more care about the transition to the coda, much of which is like the one in *Leonore II*.

Those with access to scores may be interested in some of the improvements Beethoven made in *Leonore III*. The bar-references are to *II*:

Bars 103–7: The tune is unsuited to cellos, and the players can make nothing of it; in *III* Beethoven gave it to violins and violas in triple octaves, and it sounds glorious.

142–9: This passage may look easy enough on paper, but orchestras find the rhythm almost impossible to hold even today – as any recording will demonstrate. Beethoven cut out the whole episode.

443–4: In the opening of the *presto* coda the first violins play the first subject at quadruple speed; it sounds unsatisfactory, and the composer must have thought so too.

478–501: These unrelieved syncopations are very hard to play, and ineffectual because the audience cannot hear the true beat. In *III* Beethoven brought the passage to life by syncopating only the strings and letting wind and drums play on the beat.

LEONORE I

Opera overtures were customarily written last, when the composer had the end of his opera ringing in his mind. If all Beethoven's opera had been like its latter half, *Leonore III* would have been a superb overture. But it was not; the librettist had begun with a scene of domestic comedy in the gaoler's sitting-room; the gaoler's daughter flirts with the new 'male' assistant, Fidelio, and the situation, though amusing, is slightly absurd. In 1806 Beethoven noticed that *Leonore III* killed this opening scene, and it dawned on him that his opera did not need an overture of vast intensity; it would be all the more effective with something comparatively trivial at the start. Thus it was that after writing two of the most wonderful overtures in existence he composed (presumably) two that seldom reach the concert-hall; this is a unique example of a composer rewriting because what he had written before was too good. Like its predecessors, *Leonore I* has a slow introduction, and it is a good one. The opening was probably meant to suggest Florestan's loneliness, and bars 23–4 surely represent Leonore weeping. But the main *allegro* is rather characterless. In bars 147 and 172 there are resemblances, probably unconscious, to *Leonore III*, and bars 199–200 anticipate (or recall) a memorable harmonic clash in the Violin Concerto (first movement, bar 371 etc.). This latter occurs in the only surviving quotation from Florestan's *adagio*, which is now confined to that point in the movement normally given over to development. It is in E flat and marked *adagio, ma non troppo*; in much of *Leonore III* this theme had been worked into the *allegro* in long note-values. Beethoven keeps the 'extra' bar written in *II*, which might suggest an early date, but on the repeat he cuts it as in *III*, which suggests the later one. Towards the end of the overture, he achieved a striking crescendo of the sort we associate with Rossini. But the closing bars of *Leonore I* are curiously ineffectual.

FIDELIO, OP. 72

The usual reason given for Beethoven's writing yet a fourth overture is that as revised in 1814 the opera began in a different key, A major. The *Fidelio* overture is in E, and it has been admired not so much for its effect in the concert-hall as in context in the opera-house. There is no doubt that Beethoven under-composed it with a sure sense of what was wanted. Florestan's *adagio* has now disappeared without trace. There is nothing that positively links the overture with the opera. We can, however, agree with Tovey[1] as to the Egmont-like dialogue in the slow introduction: 'A formidable power, neither good nor bad . . . alternates with a quiet pleading utterance which is soon lost in the darkness of Florestan's dungeon.' The pleading is mainly given to the horns, and it is a horn that sets the *allegro* bubbling but with a cheerful extension of the first theme. The music is terse, alive and enormously competent. After the recapitulation there is a brief return to the opening *adagio*, and the *presto* coda starts with anticipation of the finale of the Ninth Symphony (bars 843–50).

1 *Essays in Musical Analysis*, iv (London, 1936), p. 42.

The Tragedy Overtures

CORIOLAN, OP. 62

In the *Coriolan* and *Egmont* overtures Beethoven was at his most dynamic and exploratory. The earlier of the two, *Coriolan*, was written about a year after *Leonore III*, and it belongs to the same glorious period as the Fourth Piano Concerto, the Violin Concerto, and the *Razumovsky* string quartets. There is no evidence that Beethoven intended it for the theatre, though it was undoubtedly inspired by Heinrich von Collin's tragedy of that name. Collin was an Austrian civil servant and a friend of Beethoven's; his *Coriolan* had been first produced in 1802, and for three years it had been fairly popular; it then dropped out of the repertoire apart from the solitary performance mentioned below. Beethoven wrote his overture early in 1807, and as no new production was anticipated, one must presume that he happened to read the tragedy and was so moved by it that he decided to express it in music.

Newspapers, one of them as early as 8 March, mention private performances at the house of 'Prince L.', who may have been either Prince Lobkowitz or Prince Lichnowsky; they were among Beethoven's most helpful patrons, and it is quite possible that the *Coriolan* overture was given in both their palaces. Prince Lobkowitz had just become one of the directors of Vienna's Burgtheater, and he probably suggested the isolated performance there of Collin's tragedy on 24 April to test the effect of the new overture in a theatrical context. No one seems to have thought the effect so striking as to warrant further revivals.

Wagner seems to have been the first to point out that the *Coriolan* overture might just as well have been written for Shakespeare's tragedy as for Collin's, and indeed Beethoven may well have had *Coriolanus* at the back of his mind, for he possessed all Shakespeare's plays in the Eschenburg prose translation and read them constantly. Inevitably the situations must be much the same in both versions of the story, but according to Tovey the action is described rather than seen in Collin; also the hero 'finds excuses for delaying the attack upon Rome until the moment at which he can effectively commit suicide',[1] whereas in Shakespeare he is killed by the Volscians for sparing the city of his birth.

As we have seen, a theatre overture could in those days take its title from what followed without any implication that the music was 'descriptive'; with a concert overture a title is an absurdity unless the

1 Op. cit., p. 43.

music is a recognisable expression of the story. There had, of course, been earlier overtures with descriptive touches, but none had had such an all-embracing descriptive basis as Beethoven's *Coriolan*, and he felt the necessity of this because he was writing for an audience that probably knew the play but was not going to see it. As in all his best overtures, he decided to show the main conflict in the plot rather than a succession of incidents, and the main conflict lay between Coriolanus and Volumnia, between the rebel general eager to avenge his wrongs by attacking the city of his birth and his own mother pleading for mercy. C minor often seems to be Beethoven's key for passionate rebellion, and it was the key he chose for this overture. He began by depicting his hero in the fullness of his truculence and pride. There is anger both in the loud chords at the start and in the rising-quaver theme (Ex. 33*a*). The second subject represents Volumnia, and as the tender womanly phrases are repeated ever a tone higher we sense the greater urgency of her pleading. (As has been noted earlier, Beethoven uses the same chords that had served him in the First Piano Concerto for raising the pitch tone by tone: See Ex. 8.)

Beethoven is so intent on the descriptive nature of his overture that he is prepared to dispense with conventional sonata form; only the second-subject group is recapitulated. In the coda we hear Volumnia pleading yet a third time with her son, and here the switch to the minor key seems to intensify her despair. But it is at this point that her son is won over. At last the opening theme returns in C minor (Ex. 33*a*), but the truculence dissolves, to be replaced by a hopeless nullity as Coriolanus realises that any act of mercy will mean his certain death (Ex. 33*b*).

Ex. 33

The 'pedal' Cs held for four bars by oboes and bassoon in bars 145 ff. are fascinating; at several points during this passage they are quite at odds with the harmony. Later in the same year, in the slow movement of the Fifth Symphony, Beethoven gave the woodwind similarly strange 'pedal' notes towards the top of the harmony (bars 49–52 and 98–101).

EGMONT, OP. 84

Egmont was commissioned in 1809 by the Burgtheater in Vienna, together with a quantity of incidental music that included two songs for Clärchen, the heroine. The occasion was the revival of a play Goethe had written some twenty years earlier. The first performance of the new production was on 24 May 1810, but Beethoven, who had been allowed ample time for writing the music, failed to complete the overture, which was not heard until the fourth performance on 15 June. When he thought the music was about to be published, he wrote to Goethe, whom he had not then met, and promised him a copy, paying tribute to 'that glorious Egmont on which I have again reflected through you, and which I have reproduced in music as intense as my feelings when I read your play'. The subject was very close to his heart.

Count Egmont was a sixteenth-century Netherlander who resisted Spanish oppression of his country under the Duke of Alba. Despite his efforts to mediate between the Duke and the Calvinist hotheads of his own land, he was imprisoned by Alba and executed. In Goethe's tragedy Clärchen, who loves Egmont, foresees the execution and poisons herself. Egmont, sleeping in his cell, has a vision of Freedom (with Clärchen's features) who holds the victor's wreath above his head. While he is being led to execution, the orchestra plays what Goethe calls a 'victory symphony'.

Beethoven's overture uses only one theme from the incidental music: its coda is the brief 'victory symphony', without any alteration. But both the start of the *sostenuto* introduction and the second subject of the *allegro* (Ex. 34*a* & *b*) suggest the clash of wills that the plot describes, the obdurate Duke and Egmont pleading for his country; basically it is a clash between evil and good, between wrong and right, and Beethoven clearly saw it in such terms.

It will be noticed that in both cases the same rhythm serves for obduracy, and in both cases strings and woodwind are cast for the opposing roles. The overture as a whole has that extraordinary driving force that we also find in the first movement of the Fifth Symphony. The main theme of the *allegro* is on the cellos, and it falls through two octaves as though the whole fabric of Flanders were falling into limbo; the opening notes have been subtly prepared for towards the end of the slow introduction. Beethoven has total control over his material, which achieves its power to a large extent through strict economy of means. At the end of the recapitulation the obduracy rhythm rings out strikingly

Ex. 34

high on the four horns and trumpets, and the effect is unforgettable. Evil seems to have won the day. But the 'victory symphony' affirms that it has not, and with the marvellous high string writing, the addition of a piccolo, and Beethoven's complete involvement in the situation, the triumph is overwhelming.

The Later Overtures

A new theatre had long been wanted at Pest – not yet united with Buda – and in 1810 when its completion was in sight, first Collin (who refused) and then another well-known dramatist, Kotzebue, were invited to write a drama with elaborate prologue and epilogue for the opening on 4 October 1811. Kotzebue's drama, *Belas Flucht*, was scrapped and an effort by local talent substituted, but he contributed the prologue, *Ungarns erster Wohltäter* (Hungary's first benefactor, i.e. King Stephen), and epilogue, *Die Ruinen von Athen*. Beethoven, who was to provide music for them, received the text only in July 1811. During that summer he got the music written in a mere three weeks; he need not have hurried, for the first night was postponed from October until the following 10 February.

Though any new theatre in the Habsburg dominions was bound to be intended in the main for plays in German, the one in Pest was to some extent built as a concession to national feeling. Kotzebue's prologue, *König Stephan*, showed Hungary's national hero and first king, crowned in the year 1000. Stephen's chief claim to fame was his conversion of the Hungarian people to Christianity, for which he was canonised in 1083 soon after his death. The scene is an open field near Buda. Stephen's heathen subjects are converted, his Bavarian wife Gisela is welcomed by dancing children, and the misty background dissolves to reveal a vision of Buda as it would be in the future. There is a good deal of turgid dialogue in rhyming octosyllabics, five choruses, a couple of marches, and a 'melodrama' (background music behind speech, as in Act II of *Fidelio*). Nearly all the musical items are short and carelessly written.

The overture to *König Stephan* is very far from being one of Beethoven's best, but it is a good deal better than anything else in the score. The slow introduction begins enigmatically with a series of falling fourths that conceal the key and suggest a much more recent composer than Beethoven:

Ex. 35

This leads straight into a quotation from the best of the choruses, the one sung by Gisela's waiting-women. The chorus is marked *andante con moto all'ongarese*, and in the overture the Hungarian flavour is equally noticeable, with the otherwise silent first violins adding brief imitations of a cimbalom:

Ex. 36

There is some more Hungarian flavour in the exuberant quick section and one wonders how much Beethoven knew about the slow-fast contrasts of Hungarian gipsy music, familiar to us through Liszt's Hungarian Rhapsodies. The main theme is rather like that of his final chorus, though it is not the same. The second subject, one of several anticipations of the choral theme in the Ninth Symphony, is supported by a bass line in falling fourths that may or may not have been intended as a reference to the opening bars:

Ex. 37

Instead of a development section, the introductory *andante* returns: it also makes a brief appearance in the long coda, most of which is intolerably repetitive and cliché-ridden.

DIE RUINEN VON ATHEN, OP. 113

For *Die Ruinen von Athen* Beethoven wrote much more interesting incidental music, but preceded it with his worst overture. Kotzebue's libretto was boringly allegorical in a style that suggests the eighteenth rather than the nineteenth century. Athens lies in ruins under Turkish rule, and a chorus calls on 'the daughter of Zeus' for help. Minerva joyfully wakes from her 2000 years of sleep, but Mercury warns her that her 'beloved Athens' is not what it was. (Again the spoken dialogue is in rhyming octosyllabics.) Two Greek slaves are working amid the ruins of the Parthenon; dervishes, for whom Beethoven provided a delightful original chorus (even asking for improvised percussion on an unlimited scale), emerge from a mosque which was once the Temple of the Winds; janissaries pass to the music of the once-famous Turkish march – written a year or two earlier as a subject for piano variations. Minerva is horrified but Mercury assures her that the Muses have found a new home in the Germanic lands, where fresh temples have been built for them. He takes her to Pest and shows her a triumphal procession in which he points out heroes and heroines of plays by Goethe, Schiller, Lessing and Collin – Egmont and Coriolanus among them. (A stage-band alternates with the orchestra.) A temple is seen, with figures of the Muses of Tragedy and Comedy behind two altars, and in the only aria the High Priest prays for a third altar to 'our genius' (the King of Hungary, the Emperor). 'O Father Zeus,' cries Minerva, 'grant their prayer!' He does. There is a clap of thunder, and a third altar rises bearing the royal bust and inscribed 'Unserm Vater'. 'It is he,' sing the chorus ecstatically. 'We are heard!' Minerva crowns the bust with laurels, and the grateful chorus swear 'Hungarian fidelity' to the crown.

So late in a long evening the audience would have been in no mood for a lavishly designed overture; Beethoven was tactfully brief. But he began ineffectually with naïve programme music: a few bars from the melancholy duet in which the two slaves bemoan the glory that is past, followed by eight bars of the march accompanying the new glories of the modern German drama. The main *allegro* is all new, but perfunctory in form. There is a pretty tune in the middle for the woodwind with pizzicato accompaniment, but it comes only once, and there is nothing to interest in what is played before and after it.

Kotzebue did not think fit to include either of these occasional pieces in his Collected Works, but they deservedly appear in Beethoven's, for there is some interesting music amongst the rubbish. He must have enjoyed the occasion, for just before the first night he wrote to Kotzebue asking him for an opera libretto. 'I should like best of all some grand subject taken from history, and especially from the dark ages, for instance from the time of Attila or the like.' Perhaps on the lines of *King Stephen*? It is not known whether or not Kotzebue replied. Beethoven described what he wrote for Pest as his 'two little operas'. He was well aware of the limitations of his *Ruins of Athens* overture, calling it in a letter of March 1812 'a little work which can be performed in the middle of a concert as a refreshment'.

NAMENSFEIER

Beethoven never quite decided what to call his Overture in C, Op. 115. Sketches for it are spread over five years, and some of the earliest (1809) are labelled 'Overture for every occasion – or for concert use'. It may well be the first non-theatrical concert overture ever written. In 1812 Beethoven played with the notion of giving it choral parts with words from Schiller's 'Ode to Joy', but by 1814 it had become purely orchestral, perhaps an expression of relief at the apparent end of the Napoleonic Wars. The autograph score is inscribed 'Abends zum Namenstag unsers Kaisers' (evening of the Emperor's nameday, i.e. 4 October); this may indicate no more than the date of completion but the overture has generally been known as the *Namensfeier* or *Nameday* ever since. (It was published in Paris with the title 'La Chasse'.) The first performance took place on 25 December 1815, when it was played at a charity concert without any individual title.

The score shows careful workmanship but most of the themes are rather lacking in individuality, and the music is seldom heard. Beethoven had so much trouble with it that when the Edinburgh publisher, George Thomson, asked him for an overture, he told him that this was among 'the most difficult undertakings in musical composition'. A few weeks later, in April 1815, he sold this still unperformed overture, together with *König Stephan* and *Die Ruinen von Athen*, to an Austrian publisher, Steiner; he described even the last-named as a 'Grand Overture', and the contract made them Steiner's property except in England. A few weeks later still Beethoven concealed this arrangement from Charles Neate, who had come to Vienna to solicit new works for the Philharmonic Society of London. Neate returned to England with the three overtures, none of which was in Beethoven's best vein, two of which were far from new, and all of which had been sold to Steiner. The members of the Philharmonic Society were well able to distinguish good from bad, and they resigned themselves to paying for music they had no intention of performing. Meanwhile Steiner delayed bringing out the overtures, which did not appear until near the end of Beethoven's life; once again, the opus numbers are no indication of the date of composition.

Neither the music nor Beethoven's attempt to make as much money as possible out of it is to his credit. Overtures were the only category in which the quality of his music tended to deteriorate as he got older. However, his last overture, to *Die Weihe des Hauses* (*The Consecration of the House*), shows a return to something better, though not quite to Beethoven's best.

DIE WEIHE DES HAUSES, OP. 124

Die Weihe des Hauses was written in 1822, and it was his first orchestral work of any importance since the *Namensfeier* overture of seven years earlier. It was written for the opening of the Josefstadt Theatre in Vienna on 3 October. Carl Meisl had made a drastic adaptation of Kotzebue's *Ruinen* under a fresh title; Athens and the Hungarian references were eliminated. Much of the old music served well enough, though some new had to be written, and in particular Beethoven realised that the old overture would not do, especially as it would come first in the entertainment. He must have composed such new music as was required at breakneck speed, for late in September he had not started on it. Writing to his brother Johann from Baden, where he was taking 'water and bath cures', he said, 'If my health permits, I will compose another new overture' for the Josefstadt Theatre. Schindler has a story of a walk with Beethoven in the hills above Baden, during which Beethoven stopped to jot down two themes for the overture. 'He explained that he planned to develop one of them freely, and the other in the formal style of Handel . . . he had long entertained the idea of writing an overture specifically in the style of Handel.' In the overture as we have it there does not appear to be any theme subjected to 'free development'; but the Handelian one is obvious enough, though its working-out smacks a good deal more of Beethoven than of his model.

The overture is curiously constructed like a grand prelude and fugue. It begins with pomp and circumstance, *maestoso e sostenuto*, but the three sections that Beethoven strings together in his long, slow introduction (or prelude) do not seem to have anything to do with each other, and none of them recurs later. The overture begins with one of his most spacious and noble march tunes; at first it is played quietly by the woodwind with pizzicato and soft brass accompaniment, and then it is repeated very loudly by the whole orchestra. After this the trombones take no further part in the music. The next section consists of some spirited trumpeting and drumming, accompanied by extraordinary moto perpetuo semiquavers on the bassoons. The third and last section in the slow introduction is a strange, quiet fugato over a dominant pedal; the theme is rather like one in the first movement of the Ninth Symphony, a work he was writing at the same time. This eventually leads to the main *allegro*, a double fugue:

Ex. 38

Allegro con brio

Beethoven overdoes his sequence and offers no relief from these themes for more than six minutes. Nevertheless he handles them with a good deal of spirit, and on a festive occasion, such as this overture was written for, the defects would not be noticed in the general excitement of the music. This is much the best of his later overtures.

The year before he died, Beethoven had been studying Handel's *Saul*, and he told a friend: 'In future I shall write in the style of my master Handel one oratorio every year, or a concerto for some string or wind instrument – that is, when I've finished my Tenth Symphony and my Requiem.' He composed none of these works, but perhaps *The Consecration of the House* gives us an inkling of what these Handelian oratorios and concertos would have been like.

Index of Main Works Discussed

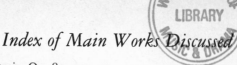